Dedication

"How much could we learn from each other if we all shared the random things that the women in our lives taught us?" I had no idea that question would lead me to hundreds of thousands of women, many of who shared their answers with me. After that TikTok video went viral, I just knew there was an opportunity to create a space where women could share wisdom from previous generations. If I'm being candid here, this was a community I've wanted to develop for years.

This book is dedicated to women who want to pass down knowledge from their grandmas and women who never had a grandma to learn from.

As young girls, we are taught to compare and compete. It's not until we're older and wiser that we realize we all hold generations of knowledge. We have so much to give to each other, starting with the things our grandmas once passed down to us.

My favorite thing about this book is that every page turn brings you into another woman's mind. Some pages provide advice about laundry and others remind us that all men are shit. When reading, you'll laugh, learn, and walk away feeling as though your cup has been filled, just as if you had visited with your grandma.

Share this book with the other women in your life. Pass it down to your daughters. Scribble in your own grandma's advice. Keep it on your nightstand or coffee table. Visit it when you need a reminder that Grandma Knows Everything.

Grandma Knows Everything

Copyright © 2023 by Amanda Ahlenius

ISBN 9798378852956

"When the price of milk is high, you can buy a gallon of whole milk and mix it ½ and ½ with reconstituted powdered milk. It will taste like 2% and is much cheaper."

"You can buy flour in bulk much cheaper than 5lb bags. Measure your flour into gallon freezer bags. Freeze them in the freezer for one week. Thaw them out. Wait for the condensation outside of the bags to dry, then place the bags into sturdy 5-gallon buckets.
The flour will stay fresh for 1 1/2 to 2 years. Make sure you have a sturdy lid on your buckets. Mice can smell grains in your pantry."

"A dirty mouth can be cleaned with a bar of brown soap."

"If somebody is bothering you, think like a goldfish. They have short-term memory."

"Beans, beans, the magical fruit. The more you eat, the more you toot."

"Nobody ever says they wish they drank more
the night before."

"Home-dried banana slices taste so much better than those flavorless store-bought things. Dip the bananas in lemon juice before drying. My great-grandchildren love my dried banana slices!"

"Never drink your bath water."

"8 oz of warm water and a teaspoon of baking soda will always relieve heartburn and painful gas.

"Always keep a handgun in the tampon box because men won't look there."

"Peanut butter will get chewing gum out of your hair."

"Save your wrappers from sticks of butter. Put them in a bag, and store them in the freezer. Then, use them to grease your baking pans."

"If you're not bad, you're not having fun."

"Add a couple drops of saline solution to your mascara or brow gel when they are almost out. You'll get a few more weeks of use out of them!"

"Add two crushed Aspirin to a hot bath to relieve period cramps."

"Put Dawn dish soap into the toilet bowl when it's clogged. You will cut the time you plunge in half."

"If you clog your ears while swimming, add a few more drops of water into your ear. Then, tilt your head so all of the water comes out."

"You don't have to cook everything on high heat."

"Do NOT get married at 20!"

"Put raw eggs in a bowl of water. If they float, they are bad."

"A great time to get a manicure is right after you put your spring garden in the ground."

"Save your fruit peels. Keep them in the freezer, then boil them when you're expecting guests. Everyone will tell you that your house smells amazing."

"Always have a separate bank account from your husband. Nobody needs to tell you how to spend your money."

"Use coffee filters to clean your glass windows."

"Use newspaper to clean your glass windows."

"Never waste a shitty day. If you get a ticket and a flat tire on the same day, pay your bills and book a gyno appointment. Do everything you hate doing on that day. Get it over with."

"Spills on the stove are much easier to clean when the stove is still warm."

"Sleep with a banana at the end of the bed to keep charlie's horses away."

"Marry rich, THEN learn to love!"

"Keep a cup of dish soap, apple cider vinegar, and water on the counter to keep fruit flies away."

"There's not much that a peanut butter sandwich and an ice-cold Coke can't fix."

"Don't marry a man with diabetes. They don't get cured. They also don't die."

"Vacuum slowly, sing often, wrap gifts with love, and make sweets for the people you like."

"Fold the front of your baby's diaper down once to prevent poop from going up and onto their stomach."

"Spray perfume on the inside of your thighs because you never know how your day will end."

"Instead of chasing eggshells around with your finger in the bowl, scoop it out with a bigger piece of shell. Shell attracts shell."

"Find a career you love, not just for the money."

"You do not have to stay with a man you love if he beats you, is emotionally abusive, or won't get off drugs for you or the kids."

"Let them go. If they come back, it's meant to be."

"Believe and love in Jesus."

"Dawn dish soap and warm water will remove oil stains from clothes."

"Instead of wallowing in what isn't going your way, say to yourself, "So, let's see what I'm made of."

"If he shows up chewing gum on the first date, send him away."

"Bedside snack cabinets are a necessity."

"A week before your menstrual cycle, your man will have his, and he will be moody."

"You haven't lived until you've put American cheese on your apple pie."

"Use distilled vinegar as a universal fabric softener."

"Always pat your face dry with a towel instead of rubbing it."

"Do not immediately answer the phone for a man. Even if you're laying in bed, act busy."

"JUST DO IT. You have to just do it."

"Hairspray can get most stains out of clothes."

"A spoonful of peanut butter will cure hiccups."

"When you're done cooking dinner, add warm water to the pan and leave it to cool. It will be much easier to clean when you do dishes."

"Always leave an extra makeup bag in the car."

"Get a job that you can support your family with. If you get a divorce or if your partner can't help, you will need to pay bills."

"Be careful what you tell your husband because men love to use things against women."

"Always make sure the water in the kitchen sink is heated up before starting the dishwasher so it runs with hot water."

"A little stubble on your legs will help keep your socks up."

"Just because it comes in your size on the rack doesn't mean it fits you!"

"Put a few drops of lavender oil into dry or clumpy mascara. It will make it good as new and will support your lashes."

"There's nothing wrong with getting coffee with anyone that isn't your man."

"Dry shampoo is just corn starch in pretty bottles."

"Be a lesbian."

"Always rinse your rice before you cook it."

"Let your cake batter sit for a few minutes so the ingredients can fully activate before you bake it."

"If you put a rosary in your bushes the night before a big event, it will bring good weather."

"After folding a towel, take a minute to smooth it flat so it stays crisp."

"Butter the bread before you make a peanut butter and jelly sandwich to keep the peanut butter from sticking to your throat."

"Men are shit. All of them."

"When people talk about you, they're leaving someone else alone."

"If your sugar is as hard as a rock, throw a piece of bread into the bag."

"Place a penny on a bee sting to relieve pain."

"A damp rag will get all the lint off of clothes."

"Dogs chase cars, not women! Women shouldn't chase dogs!"

"You have to be a tourist in your own town."

"If you're putting cash into a birthday card, flat iron the bills so they're crisp and presentable."

"If you don't want to have any more children, wash your underwear separately from your husband's."

"Put a storebought cake on a plate of your own. Poke it with a spoon a few times and blot it with a paper towel. It will look homemade."

"Lather shampoo in your hand until it turns white before you use it on your hair."

"Febreeze your mirrors and metal to make them shine."

"Don't let a fool kiss you, and don't let a kiss fool you."

"Eat delicious food. One day you could get hit by a bus."

"Don't tattoo a guy's name on your body, or your whole body will be covered."

"Soda is a good remedy for an upset stomach."

"Sana, sana, colita de rana."

"If you don't use it, you'll lose it. You know exactly what I'm trying to say."

"Wash your whites with vinegar and a drop of Dawn blue dish soap. Then, dry them in the sun."

"Marry the man that loves you more than you could ever love them."

"A little 'after dinner' ice cream and Wheel of Fortune is a good night."

"If you need to wash your stuffed animals, put them in a pillowcase and tie the ends to keep the fur from getting damaged."

"Don't ride in the back of a truck unless your hair is pulled back."

"If you're having a hard time making a decision, just make one. You want to be a woman who knows what she wants."

"Write your name and date on everything you create."

"Rub a bar of soap on your doors if they're getting stuck in the frame."

"If your makeup feels too dry, mix a serum or moisturizer with your foundation."

"If something is stuck to a pan, let it soak with a dryer sheet."

"Put a cup of iodine salt in the washer with your colored clothing to prevent the colors from bleeding together."

"Wipe your hands on stainless steel to rid them of the smell of onion."

"Always reheat your pizza in a frying pan, not the oven."

"Keep a clean basket near the front door just to collect clutter if someone stops by."

"Put a teaspoon of rice in your salt shaker to keep the salt from clumping."

"You can't poop? Eat apples and drink coffee."

"When wearing pearls, put them on last and take them off first. This will prevent them from being damaged."

"Always buy Toyota or Honda."

"Flip your hangers backward, then put laundry away normally. Every 6 months or so go through your wardrobe to see which hangers haven't been turned around. Donate those clothes."

"Live like you're poor, and you'll be rich."

"Always wear underwear because sometimes women can leave a trail."

"Don't submerge wooden spoons or cutting boards in water."

"A wise woman always keeps a 'nest egg' that nobody else knows about."

"Rub parchment paper on your shower rod to make the rings move smoother when opening and closing the curtain."

"If you're out of vanilla extract, just use maple syrup."

"Olive oil is great for removing makeup."

"Chewed tobacco leaves are the best things to get a bee stinger out."

"Leave the avocado pits in your guacamole to prevent it from turning brown."

"Always dust your hands with flour before you touch your dough."

"If you need to clean your eraser, just rub it on your jeans."

"Put eyedrops on your pimples to reduce redness and inflammation."

"How he treats his mother is how he will treat you."

"If you burn your skin, rub cold mustard on it to neutralize the pain."

"If the meat you're cooking isn't tender, throw a spoon into the pot while it finishes cooking."

"The only reason you need to learn the rules is so you know how to break them."

"If you get tree sap on yourself, rub butter on it."

"A dollar bill is 6 inches long. You can use it as a ruler when you're in a pinch."

"Splash a little bit of vinegar into the pan when you're cooking ground beef to get the smell out of the kitchen."

"If your knitted clothes shrink in the dryer, fill a sink with cold water and pull it in and out of the water to stretch it back out."

"Don't wash your windows on sunny days. It makes them streaky."

"The tag of a bedsheet always goes in the back right corner of the bed."

"When you're feeling sick, cut a potato into slices and put them in your socks before you go to bed."

"Brush your hair starting from the bottom.
Then work your way up."

"Eating carrots will improve your eyesight.
Eating bread crust will make your hair curly."

"Here is how to make the best white rice: after 7 minutes of medium heat, put aluminum foil over the pan and reduce the heat to low until the rice is done."

"Always have your own money."

"Dish soap and a little scrubbing works better than detergent to remove stains."

"Succinylcholine doesn't show up in an autopsy."

"As a rule, a man is a fool. When it's hot, he wants it cool. When it's cool, he wants it hot. He always wants what he hasn't got."

"Don't add water to the pot when making cabbage or sweet potatoes."

"Marry for love the first time. Marry for money the second time."

"Never start a fight, but always finish it."

"Store your berries in mason jars to make them last a few more weeks."

"A spoonful of sugar gets rid of hiccups."

"The less you touch your pie crust before baking, the better it turns out."

"Always eat well. Whether it's a good or bad day."

"Crush up Benadryl and put it on your canker sores. They will be gone tomorrow."

"Banana peels whiten your teeth!"

"Dab sparkling water into a stain to prevent it from settling in."

"Every problem has a solution."

"Three things belong in the freezer: pantyhose, batteries, and tequila."

"Always stare at yourself in the mirror and picture a younger version of you. Adore yourself."

"Even a free bird needs to eat a worm every now and then."

"Wine and cheese is definitely dinner."

"Cut your onions on top of wet paper towels to prevent tears."

"If you're drying shoes, trap the shoelaces in the door so they're not banging around in the dryer."

"Do NOT get up and sit in a chair right after you have a baby."

"PineSol takes the mildew smell out of towels and shoes."

"Baby oil and olive oil are great shaving cream substitutes."

"Never let a man make a fool of you more than once. They will become too comfortable with disrespecting you."

"Throw PineSol in the sink a few minutes before the man comes home so it smells like you've been cleaning."

"Put baking soda on bee stings."

"The best chocolate chip cookie recipe: Bake premade cookie dough at 350F for 10-20 minutes, then freeze for 10 more minutes."

"Put 'like with like' when organizing things."

"Never cook for a man you don't plan to keep."

"More souls are MADE than saved at church camp."

"Put butter in the water when you're boiling starches to stop the water from boiling over."

"Don't ever let your purse touch the ground."

"Don't watch a dog pee or you'll get a stye in your eye. Also, never cry into the wind."

"Wash your underwear with fragrance and dye-free detergent if you're prone to yeast infections."

"Tap a butter knife around a lid when it's too tight to open."

"If it's at an antique store, it's haunted."

"Don't sleep with a bra on."

"Use a black piece of clothing to rub deodorant stains out of your shirt."

"If you're having trouble determining whether or not to say 'me and her' or 'she and I,' break it up. "I went to the store," not "Me when to the store."

"Use dating as a chance to gather data, not fall in love."

"Fake the pie, not the O."

"Never fall for the guy with the nice sports car."

"Don't trouble trouble unless trouble troubles you."

"Don't have just one man. Be like Jesus and love them all."

"It's good enough for who it's for."

"Vaseline is a natural lash and eyebrow serum."

"You can get crayon and candle wax off hardwood floors with a blow dryer. Heat up the stain until it melts, then wipe clean."

"When you're trying to put a baby to sleep, gently blow on their face. They will close their eyes."

"Throw a spaghetti noodle at the wall while cooking. If it sticks, it's done."

"Bread lasts 10x longer in the refrigerator."

"Drink sugar water after a traumatic experience to calm your nerves."

"Behind every great man is a woman who made them that way."

"There can only be one crazy one in the relationship, and that crazy one better be you."

"Clean glass doors up and down on the inside and side to side on the outside. Then you always know which side has the streak."

"You are lucky to live in a time where women can be independent and make money. Travel the world and never take that for granted."

"No answer is an answer."

"Every person has faults so pick the faults you can live with and stay with. You're not perfect either."

"The biggest investment you should make for yourself is a good mattress for better sleep and a good pair of shoes."

"Light a match after you use the restroom to cover up the smell."

"Clear nail polish will stop the run in your stockings."

"Always keep Butterfingers in the fridge for a nice cold treat."

"Hairspray will keep your bathing suit bottoms in place."

"Buy nice things and also take care of them."

"Always carry your wallet in your front pocket."

"Only use enough wrapping paper to cover the gift you're wrapping."

"Red wine stains can be removed with a little hydrogen peroxide and dawn dish soap."

"Women can make their own money."

"If you're walking somewhere and feel threatened, walk towards a house with toys in the yard. There's probably a mom there."

"Freeze your vegetable scraps. Then, use them with chicken bones to make broth."

"Put chocolate pudding mix into your favorite brownie batter recipe. It will make you famous."

"When a glass breaks, use a piece of bread to clean up all of the scraps."

"A body in motion stays in motion."

"1 cup of milk and 1 tbsp of lemon juice = buttermilk. 1 cup of milk and ⅓ cup of butter = heavy cream."

"Hang a towel partly out of the dishwasher while it's running. You won't have to dry the dishes when it's done."

"Independence is a power."

"Don't pour pasta into your strainer. Instead, put the strainer over the pot, then flip it."

"Put a penny in your flower vase to revive your flowers."

"If you think you're ready to have kids, put a glass of water between your legs and try walking around with it."

"Fill a sock up with salt, then heat it up in the microwave. Place it on your chest to break up mucus."

"Put your dish sponges in the microwave to kill the bacteria."

"If trauma can be passed down from generation to generation, so can love, knowledge, and community."

Thank you, Grandmas.

Join the Grandma Knows Everything community!

Find Amanda Ahlenius on TikTok.

Made in the USA
Middletown, DE
09 June 2023

32329829R00130